Revised Edition

Confederate Camp Cooking

Patricia B. Mitchell

Copyright © 1990, 1991 by Patricia B. Mitchell.

Published 1991 by the author at Mitchells Publications,
P. O. Box 429, Chatham, VA 24531.
   Telephone/fax: 434-432-0595
   Book Sales: 800-967-2867
   E-mail: answers@foodhistory.com
   Website: www.foodhistory.com

Printed in the U. S. A.
ISBN 0-925117-46-3

Thirteenth Printing, June 2004

- Illustrations -

Center Front Cover - adapted from an illustration provided by Dover Publications, Inc., New York.

Inside Title Page, Back Cover, and Front Cover Corners - by Henry H. Mitchell.

Inside Back Cover - portrait of the author by David L. Mitchell.

Table of Contents

Introduction 1

"... The Troops ... Were Without ..." 2
    Skillet Salmon Patties...................................3
    Salmon and Green Peas Under Biscuits..............4
    Scalloped Salmon and 'Taters.........................5
    Parched Corn...10
    Foragers' Potato Soup................................12
    "Then" Potato Soup...................................12
    "Now" Potato Soup....................................13
    Confederate Corn Chowder..........................13
    Messmate Tomato-Corn Soup.......................13
    Fish Chowder..14
    Quick Fix Fish Bisque.................................14
    Mock Oyster Stew......................................14
    What-Have-You Stew..................................15
    "Beef Tea. Receipt for 6 Pints"....................15
    "To Boil Dried Peas"..................................16
    Green Hill Beans.......................................16
    Battlefield Baked Beans...............................16
    Sesame Seed Skillet Corn Bread....................18
    Dixie Corn Dodgers...................................19
    Campfire Corn Bread..................................20
    No-Flour Camp Corn Bread.........................20
    Corncakes..21
    Swedish Hardtack......................................23
    Southern Soda Crackers...............................23
    Cush I...28
    Cush II..28
    Cush III...28
    8th Virginia Jerky Recipe............................30
    Peanut-Pea Salad.......................................32
    Wilted Greens with
        Sweet/Sour Bacon Dressing....................33
    "Discovered Garden" Rice...........................33
    Sassafras Beer..34
    Roasted Rat...35

Notes...35

Introduction

"It is well war is so terrible, or we should get too fond of it," General Robert E. Lee declared to General W. N. Pendleton while they watched the repulse of over 100,000 Federal troops at Fredericksburg.[1]

Cavalryman Timothy E. Mitchell wrote to his wife Ardelia on December 12, 1863, "When I entered the service I expected to fight. I shall continue to do so while I have breath. When that stops, I shall cease to shoot — not that I think there is much justice in this war, but I consider it my duty to fill a soldier's position while I am one — we have a good army here, but the world cannot produce a better army than the Yankees. . . ."[2]

The typical Southern soldier was not a starry-eyed dreamer with unrealistic expectation of "whipping the Yankees" in a few days or weeks. He was, however, a courageous man committed to the cause of defending his homeland, no matter what the cost. This high level of commitment on the part of the Confederate soldier was evident not only in his willingness to face the danger of enemy ammunition, but also in his resignation to the boredom and sparsity of army life and diet; and in his calm acceptance of the fact that camp life often meant camp diseases: dysentery, typhoid fever, pneumonia, measles, chicken pox, raging infections. Of the approximately 300,000 Southern men who died in the War Between the States, nearly two-thirds succumbed to camp diseases. The soldier's dedication to the war effort was also evidenced by his ready sacrifice of the joys of living with wife and offspring in exchange for the companionship of often lice-infested, smelly, tobacco-chewing "Butternuts."

The purpose of this book is to explore the life-style of the Southern soldier, with a special emphasis on the food he ate ("such as it was, and what there was of it"). We will look at his rations, and his culinary improvisations. Authentic Civil War era recipes and commemorative recipes will be presented. These recipes will be of great interest to amateur historians and cooking enthusiasts, but most especially to Confederate re-enactors who may wish to use some of the "receipts" at Civil War encampments.

". . . The Troops . . . Were Without . . ."

Napoleon stated that an army marches on its stomach; and due largely to his offering a prize (12,000 francs, or the modern equivalent of a quarter of a million dollars) for the discovery of a way to get better food to the French army, the process of hermetically sealing food for future use was invented in 1795 by a French confectioner, Nicholas Appert. In 1810, a patent was taken out in England for Appert's method, and soon the idea spread to America where salmon and lobster were the first foods canned. In 1823 an American, Thomas Kensett, invented the tin can. By 1861, meats, poultry, fish, vegetables, fruit, and milk were being sold in cans. To an army, canned products were advantageous in that the foods, of course, kept well and were easily transported.

The South, however, did not utilize canned products during the Civil War to the extent that the North did, because the agriculturalized Confederacy lacked the factories and food processing plants of the North. A shortage of shipping containers also plagued the South. As far as the transportation of food (be it canned, in barrels, in crates, or whatever) was concerned, the Confederate States were at a further disadvantage because, as the war wore on, the railroad transportation network in Dixie was breaking down. This problem was brought about not only by Union soldiers' making "pretzels" out of railroad tracks, but also by the inefficiency of many of the agents and officers assigned to facilitate the proper distribution of supplies impressed from the citizens.

By 1864, Cooper DeLeon could report from Richmond:

> *"No department was worse neglected and mismanaged than the Transportation Department. The existence of the Virginia army wholly depended on a single line, close to the coast and easily tapped. Nor did the Government's seizure of its control in any manner remedy the evil. Often and again, the troops around Richmond were without beef — once for 12 days at a time; they were often without flour, molasses or salt, living for days upon cornmeal alone; and the ever-ready excuse was want of transportation.*
>
> *"Thousands of bushels of grain would ferment and rot at one station; hundreds of barrels of meat stacked at another, while the army starved because [of] 'no transportation.'"* [3]

Nevertheless, canned products were sometimes available to the Southern soldier thanks to blockade runners or the capture of Union supplies. French imported salmon, green peas, and sardines were thought to be more appetizing than American goods such as canned condensed milk, meats, oysters, and vegetables. The following recipes use salmon and green peas in simple casseroles which possibly are similar to concoctions actually prepared in camp. (Men on the march, of course, had no time for even easy recipes; foods were consumed raw or cooked in the simplest manner possible. A sardine sandwich might have been an option; sardines on hardtack would have been hard for even the strongest digestive system — and teeth — to tackle!)

Skillet Salmon Patties

For every one cup of canned salmon, add two beaten eggs, one cup soft bread crumbs, two tablespoons minced onion, and salt and pepper to taste. Mix well; form into patties; and sauté in butter in a heavy skillet. Turn once to lightly brown both sides.

Salmon and Green Peas Under Biscuits

2 tbsp. butter
2 tbsp. onion, minced (optional)
2 tbsp. flour
1 c. milk
Salt and pepper
2 c. canned green peas, drained
1 c. canned salmon, drained (tuna could be used)

For the convenience of today's cook, one can of cream of mushroom soup can be substituted for the first five ingredients.

Melt the butter in a saucepan. Sauté onion, blend in flour, and cook, stirring for several minutes. Gradually add the milk, stirring out the lumps.

Cook until thickened. Add salt, pepper, peas, and salmon. Stir. Spoon into a 1 1/2 - quart casserole dish. Meanwhile, prepare drop biscuit batter from the following Master Mix recipe. (Note: this makes superb biscuits which can be eaten separately! Just mix up a larger quantity of batter, using the same ratio of oil and milk to dry ingredients.)

Master Biscuit Mix

4 c. whole wheat flour
4 c. unbleached or all-purpose flour
1/3 c. baking powder
1 tbsp. salt

Mix all ingredients (store in refrigerator or freezer for later use, if desired).[4]

To complete preparation of the Salmon and Green Peas Under Biscuits recipe, take 1 1/2 c. of Master Biscuit Mix and add 3/4 c. milk and 2 tbsp. vegetable oil. Mix. With a large spoon, drop mounds of batter on top of the salmon/pea mixture. Bake uncovered at 425° F. for about 15 minutes, or until the biscuit tops start to brown. Serves 4 to 6. If desired, sprinkle on paprika or grated cheddar cheese.

Scalloped Salmon and 'Taters

Grease a large casserole dish. Meanwhile, combine one can of salmon, partly drained; one can cream of mushroom soup (or one c. medium-thickness white sauce); one c. chopped onion; a dash of salt and pepper; 1 tbsp. prepared mustard; and 2-3 c. cooked sliced potatoes. (Add salmon liquid if the mixture is too thick.) Spoon into the casserole dish and bake covered at 375° F. for 30 minutes. Serves 4 generously.

Fishing was another way the troops in camp acquired food, and oysters in the shell roasted on the fire were a treat where and when available.

Successful foraging, if the locality was not already "eaten out," might have produced Irish potatoes. Sweet potatoes were another hunger-killer enjoyed by the men in gray. Both sweet potatoes and corn in the husks were frequently roasted in the coals of the campfire.

The question of availability of food in the countryside near the soldiers' camp was of great concern to every man in the Southern army. Capt. C. M. Blackford of Co. B, 2nd Va. Cavalry, wrote to his wife from Bunker Hill, Virginia, on October 14, 1862:

> *"We have only poor beef to eat, and that without salt, and flour without lard, salt or soda, with which to cook our biscuits. This country has been laid waste. Even the green corn out in the fields has been used up. What the people are to do I do not know."* [6]

Two descriptions which follow detail how the civilian population would often, when possible, feed the soldiers in their area. First is an account from Capt. Blackford describing the fortuitous events of the morning of June 5, 1861, while his unit was passing through Nelson County, Virginia, on their way to Manassas:

"About daylight the next morning I was awakened by a messenger bringing me a note from Mr. and Mrs. Jesse L. Heiskell who lived a mile or two north of the Rockfish and directly on our road asking me to extend an invitation to the whole command to breakfast with them. It was joyous news as we had no place to cook and nothing to cook if we had a place. The men were soon up and more than usual time was given for washing and dressing for everyone wanted to look as spry as possible. The sun came out very brightly and it was an ideal day. When everybody was washed and brushed and dry again we started out with longing appetites and reached the house about eight o'clock. In the lot adjoining his barn we found ample provender for our horses and the house was one vast dining-room. I was put in command of the entertainment. On the porch there were three or four tubs of mint julep, over which I placed a guard with orders not to allow more than one drink without my permission. While the men were being served the officers went into breakfast, and such a breakfast for hungry men! Everything known to Virginia housekeepers was there, and in such abundance that the last relief that went into breakfast had just as much and just as good as was served to the officers at the first table. I hurried through and divided the men up into reliefs, putting each relief under the charge of a sergeant, and then the reliefs were taken into breakfast successively.

"The exploit in housekeeping I have never known equalled. Mrs. Heiskell told me she had heard of our arrival at the river about bedtime and had determined to give us a breakfast. Couriers were sent out to the neighbors and they rapidly assembled, bringing chickens, eggs, butter, ham and every possible delicacy; then with their cooks they set to work and by daylight the bountiful supply for two hundred men, of which we so joyfully partook, was ready.

"When all had eaten to repletion the squadron was formed in front of the house, sabres presented, three cheers given, and I returned thanks in the name of the command. We wheeled into column and marched away very gay and happy." [6]

Capt. Blackford's wife reported the following hospitality to visiting soldiers witnessed in Hanover County, Virginia, in 1863:

"I remember a charming visit to Dewberry, the residence of Mrs. Edmonia Cooke .... The house was full of company, principally of young ladies .... Of the many military beaux whom we found there, visitors from Pickett's division, many were to be left dead upon the field after the glorious charge that division made at Gettysburg.

"I can ever remember the simple elegance of the house, the cordial hospitality, the delicious dinner served, and my recollection, sharpened doubtless by my scant fare in camp, especially recurs to an elegant quarter of mutton dressed with drawn butter, eggs and green pickle. I am sure there never was such a delicious piece of meat. I remember also the lovely face and gracious manner of old Mrs. Cooke and how she made us feel the sincerity of her welcome . . . . " [7]

In discussing his family's situation and food availability at the end of the "War of Northern Aggression," Capt. Blackford tells of receiving his first fee for legal work:

> ". . . Each laid down a half-dollar and walked out. I was amazed at my wealth, seized it, closed the office and went home to show the spoils to my wife. . . . With part of it we bought our first herring and a slice of cheese. No one can tell how good a herring and a piece of cheese is until they have had none for four years." [8]

In camp in the winter, when there was less fighting and marching, the soldiers' diet became more varied and tasty. The commissary, which often fell behind the troops when the army was rapidly advancing usually could, in the winter days of wait-and-see, provide somewhat better supplies to the men. However, the quality of the food even then was not necessarily good. Beef and pork were notoriously inferior. "Sowbelly" (salt pork) and "salt horse" (pickled beef) were often issued to the troops. (The army diet was, in fact, built around fried salt pork — sometimes even eaten raw when desperate hunger hit; hardtack; and coffee, or a substitute.) Parched corn, goober peas (peanuts), and jerky were other "on the march" foods. Fresh meat was occasionally issued to the men, especially in the winter; and sometimes they acquired fresh meat by hunting game or by appropriating cattle which they encountered. Another source of supplies was provided by Southern women who smuggled goods into camp under the cover of hoop skirts and voluminous petticoats. These individuals hid contraband articles in their clothing and then sold them to needy soldiers at a nice profit. A Mrs. Roger A. Pryor reported an incident in Blackwater, Virginia. A female rode into camp. Beneath her outer garments were concealed, "a roll of army cloth, several pairs of cavalry boots, a roll of crimson flannel, packages of gilt braid and sewing thread, cans of preserved meat, a bag of coffee." [9]

The following description of camp conditions was written by James J. McDonald at the turn of the century in his book *Life in Old Virginia*.

"It is stated that after the first year of the war, the daily rations of a Confederate soldier when marching or fighting, were one pint of cornmeal, one-fourth pound of bacon. If camping, in addition to this he drew one-fourth pound of sugar, or one-half pint of molasses, three-fourths of a pound of black peas, one ounce of salt, and one-eighth of a pound of soap, and on Christmas Day, a 'jagger of pinetop whiskey.'

"When Confederate General E. Kirby Smith invaded Kentucky in 1862, his army had ten days' rations issued to them and started afoot over the mountains to get in the rear of Cumberland Gap. At the end of the sixth day, there were not six pounds of rations in the whole division. In order to supply his men with something to eat, he bought whole fields of corn, which were in the roasting ear stage, and his soldiers were told to help themselves. Having left their wagon and supply train behind with their cooking utensils, they were obliged to build fires to roast the corn, the result being that it was burned black on the outside and raw on the inside. An ex-Confederate soldier told the writer that his daily ration for more than a week before the surrender at Appomattox, was an ear of corn for himself and three for his horse." [10]

Parched corn was also a common food among the soldiers. It is prepared as follows:

Parched Corn

Pick extremely mature ears of sweet corn, the kernels of which are easily removed. (If the ears are not dried out enough, pull back the husks of the corn, tie the ears in bunches, and hang to dry.) When the corn is dry, parch the kernels in a hot covered skillet containing a small amount of fat. Keep the lid on until the popping stops, and shake frequently. Remove the corn when the kernels are golden brown.

Drain on paper towels, if available, and add salt to taste.

Another Virginian (and Confederate doctor), John H. Claiborne, wrote the following comments:

"Rations were light, provisions of all sorts scarce, luxuries unknown, and clothing without suspicion of style or fashion. Cut off by the blockade from foreign supplies, we were dependent upon home resources, already overtaxed and imperfect, for almost everything. Only cornbread, peas, and sorghum were plentiful. The latter took the place of molasses, and at the same time was known as 'long sweetening,' in the place of sugar, for our coffee, which consisted of parched rye or dried sweet potatoes. It was also the saccharine element of the 'pies' . . . , they being the first investment from his meagre pay. Only the blockade runners, or their intimate friends, could indulge in the luxuries of eating, and drinking, or in the display of fine clothes." [11]

Some of the items smuggled in were not the latest fashions from Paris, of course, but rather necessary and/or useful goods which benefited the Confederate soldier and civilian. Early in 1864, President Jefferson Davis was given by Congress sole authority over the shipment of cotton. At this point, a Bureau of Foreign Supplies was established to sell cotton for the Confederacy. This plan was quite successful, bringing about the import (through the Yankee blockade) of 500,000 pairs of shoes, 69,000 rifles, 316,000 blankets, 2,000,000 pounds of saltpeter, 800,000 pounds of bacon, and various other supplies just during the last three months of 1864.[12]

Capt. Charles M. Blackford reported from camp in Virginia on June 7, 1864:

> *"We are eating new beautiful onions from Nassau — whether raised in Connecticut or not I cannot say — they are imported at Wilmington [NC]. With our onions we have bacon cured in Ohio and shipped to Nassau to be sent us by blockade runners."* [13]

Even when supplies were available, sufficient quantities of pots and pans were not to be had. One Southern colonel declared in 1863, "I cannot fight more until I get something to cook in!" [14]

Because of these handicaps, the Confederate who was in charge of meals (the soldiers ofttimes selected one man to do the cooking for groups of five to ten other men) could only provide meals based upon what foodstuffs happened to be on hand and on his own personal creativity. Soups and stews were a way to add variety to the sometimes daily pattern of beans and cornbread. The following recipes demonstrate and commemorate some ingenious camp-style dishes.

Foragers' Potato Soup

3 c. peeled, diced potatoes
2 c. water
3/4 tsp. salt
1 c. onion, chopped
2 tbsp. vegetable oil or butter
2 tbsp. flour
2 c. milk
1 tsp. dried parsley
1/2 to 1 tsp. garlic powder
1/4 tsp. pepper

Bring potatoes, water, and salt to a boil in a saucepan. Reduce heat and simmer, covered, for 15 minutes or until the potatoes are tender. Without draining the potatoes, mash them up.

Meanwhile, in a large saucepan, heat oil and add onion. Sauté until the onion is soft. Sprinkle in flour, and stir for one minute. Gradually add the milk, stirring frequently for 5 or 10 minutes until thickened.

Add cooked potato mixture and seasonings, blending together. Serves four to six persons.

"Then" Potato Soup

"Mash potatoes, pour on them one teacup cream, one large spoonful butter.

"Pour boiling water on them till you have the desired quantity. Boil until it thickens, season with salt, parsley and pepper to your taste." [15]

"Now" Potato Soup

Bring to a boil:

2 tbsp. onion flakes or 1 onion, minced
1/2 tsp. celery seeds
1/2 tsp. salt
1/2 tsp. dry parsley
Dash of pepper
Dash of garlic powder
4 c. milk

Add:

1 1/2 c. potato flakes (or enough to make soup the thickness you like))

Confederate Corn Chowder

3 c. water
1 medium onion, diced
1 c. potato flakes
1 c. whole kernel corn
1/2 c. dry milk powder
Salt and pepper

Combine ingredients in a large pot. Bring to a boil and simmer until the onion is tender. Season to taste. Makes 6 servings.

Messmate Tomato-Corn Soup

2 c. chicken broth (or 2 chicken bouillon cubes in 2 c. boiling water)
2 c. canned tomatoes, cut up
2 c. whole kernel corn (drained, if canned)
1/4 tsp. salt
1/4 tsp. marjoram, basil, or oregano if available
Dash of pepper

Boil up. Simmer, uncovered, for 15 minutes.

Fish Chowder

"Fry a few slices of salt pork, cut the fish in small pieces, pare and slice . . . [some] potatoes; add a little onion chopped fine.

"Place all in layers in the kettle, season with salt and pepper. Stew over a slow fire thirty minutes." [16]

Quick Fix Fish Bisque

1 tbsp. vegetable oil
1 medium onion, diced
2 tbsp. flour
4 c. canned tomatoes, chopped up, undrained
2 tsp. dried parsley
2 1/2 c. milk
1/2 lb. fish fillets, cut into 1/2-inch chunks
Salt and pepper to taste
2 tsp. garlic powder

Heat the oil in a large pot. Add the onions and cook until the onion is translucent. Blend in flour. Add remaining ingredients. Bring to a boil, lower heat, cover, and simmer until the fish is flaky, stirring occasionally.

Mock Oyster Stew

3 tbsp. butter or margarine
5 tbsp. flour
4 c. milk, warmed
Onion powder
Celery seeds
Salt and pepper
1 can water-packed tuna, undrained
Oyster or soda crackers

Melt the fat; blend in flour. Gradually stir in milk, cooking until thickened. Season. Add broken-up tuna. Heat and serve with crackers.

What-Have-You Stew

The name says it all! In a large pot dump the contents of cans of tomatoes, vegetables, meats — whatever you like. Add water, chopped onions, seasonings (especially cayenne pepper, a Civil War - era favorite) and boil up. Simmer until you and your "messmates" are ready to dine — mighty fine!

"Beef Tea. Receipt for 6 Pints"

"Cut three pounds of beef into pieces the size of walnuts, and chop up the bones, if any; put it into a convenient-sized kettle, with 1/2 pound of mixed vegetables, such as onions, leeks, celery, turnips, carrots (or one or two of these, if all are not to be obtained), one ounce of salt, a little pepper, one teaspoonful of sugar, two ounces of butter, half a pint of water. Set it on a sharp fire for ten minutes or a quarter of an hour, stirring now and then with a spoon, till it forms a rather thick gravy at bottom, but not brown; then add seven pints of hot or cold water, but hot is preferable; when boiling, let it simmer gently for an hour, skim off all the fat, strain it through a sieve, and serve." [17]

The camp cook did have to rely on beans and cornbread to feed his messmates when more diverse foods were not available. Actually, from a nutritional point of view, this is a commendable combination because the incomplete protein of legumes and corn together make complete protein. Also, if one is not bored with a monotonous diet of beans and cornbread, that menu makes for good eating! — A quote of the period advises eating plenty of cornfield peas (blackeyed peas) because they are beneficial to your general health of mind and body, a dish of which "fattens you up, makes you sassy, goes throo and throo your very soul." [18] Old instructions for the preparation of dried peas or beans read this way:

"To Boil Dried Peas"

"Soak in boiling water the night before. Then next day parboil and drain. Put in fresh water with a piece of middling or ham, and boil until tender." [19]

A sad story from the War for Southern Independence was told by a Federal officer after the battle of Chattanooga. He had found the body of a thin Tennessee lad lying barefoot in the cold, a day's rations in the haversack: "A handful of black beans, a few pieces of sorghum and half a dozen roasted acorns" — a sorry ration for a man who probably could have burned 5,000 or more calories a day.[20]

The following recipes are updated modes of preparing beans.

Green Hill Beans

1 large-size can baked beans
1/4 - 1/3 c. brown sugar, packed
1 tsp. dry mustard

Combine ingredients. Bake at 325° F. for 2 hours.

Battlefield Baked Beans

2 16-oz. cans pork and beans
1/2 c. brown sugar (more or less, to suit your taste)

2 tbsp. dry mustard
1/2 c. tomato catsup
6 slices uncooked bacon, cut in pieces

Combine the first four ingredients in a large casserole dish. Top with bacon. Bake uncovered at 325° F. for two and a half hours. (If it gets dry, cover with foil.)

With the beans (or sometimes even without the beans) corn bread became a camp staple. Dr. Francis Porcher praised corn bread and presented the following recipe in his classic Confederate handbook, ***Resources of the Southern Fields and Forests:***

>*"In our armies, it is a universal subject of complaint that cornmeal, or flour, is not given to the soldiers in place of wheat, as it is nutritious and much more easily and better cooked. Besides, the Southern soldier is for the most part more accustomed to corn bread. The **'Boston Brown Bread,'** a useful hygienic preparation, contains two parts of corn to one part of rye meal, and is made in the following manner:*
>
>*"To three quarts of mixed meal are added a gill of molasses, two teaspoonfuls of salt, one teaspoonful of saleratus, and either a teacupful of home brewed or half a teacupful of Brewer's Yeast. This bread continues good and wholesome as long as any other bread is usually kept; but like other preparations, it is preferred warm, and is generally eaten fresh, or after being toasted. Like all other kinds of cornbread, it is an acceptable substitute not only for the bread made of other grains, but for the vegetables which use has made desirable at the noonday meal."* [21]

[Note:] "Until the end of the 18th century the only way to make baked goods light was to beat air into the dough, along with eggs, or to add yeast or spirits. Then, in the 1790's, pearlash was discovered in America [produced by burning wood]. Pearlash is potassium carbonate; it produces carbon dioxide in baking dough and makes it rise . . . . An improvement on pearlash, and on saleratus, or baking soda, was baking powder, first produced commercially in the 1850's by Preston & Merrill of Boston." [22] *[This commercial baking powder did not, however, become widely available until the late 1860's.]*

The next recipes represent 20th-century cornmeal-made products in honor of the importance of cornmeal to the 19th-century men in gray.

Sesame Seed Skillet Corn Bread

3 tbsp. toasted sesame seeds
3/4 c. cornmeal
3/4 c. flour
1 tbsp. baking powder
1/2 tsp. salt
2 tbsp. vegetable oil
1 c. milk
1 egg, beaten
1 c. grated Cheddar cheese

Combine the first five ingredients. In a separate bowl, mix together the next three ingredients. Combine the two mixtures and stir in cheese. Spoon into a large greased skillet and bake at 400° F. for approximately 20 minutes.

Dixie Corn Dodgers

Coarse, gritty, and full-of-corn-flavor Dixie Corn Dodgers are bona fide camp fare. Whether cooked over a campfire or over the electric burner of a stove, they are good, solid sustenance.

2 c. cornmeal
1/2 tsp. salt
2 tsp. baking powder
2 tbsp. vegetable oil, melted butter, or bacon drippings
2/3 c. milk, approximately

Combine the dry ingredients. Stir in liquids. Form eight "bullet-shaped" dodgers. Drop in a greased and heated heavy skillet. Brown on one side, then turn to brown the bottom.

The following report shows how corn breads helped to keep one young homeward-bound Rebel, Johnny Wickersham, alive.

"... The boat pulled off, leaving me lying there on the levee bank. A Negro woman found me and took me to her cabin. Poor woman, she had nothing but corn-cake and dried pumpkin, but she gave me freely of it, and would go with me when I became able to walk, to the landing place, and as boats landed would plead with them to take me aboard, only to be refused. I had no money, and no hope.

"After weeks of her motherly nursing I felt much better, and one day told her I was going to walk to Missouri. 'No, honey, don't try it. You sure will die if you do,' was her advice. However, with a big hoecake, the only provision which she had made for me, I started on that long, weary *tramp over a country that had been ravished by both armies, and in which not a building or so much as a fence, or head of stock remained."* [23]

Other cornmeal recipes that Johnny Wickersham (and other Johnny Rebs) would have appreciated include the following.

Campfire Corn Bread

1 c. cornmeal
1 c. flour
2 tsp. baking powder
3/4 tsp. salt
1 c. milk
1/4 c. vegetable oil

Mix dry ingredients. Stir in liquids. Spoon into a well-greased, heated 10- or 12-inch skillet. Cover tightly. Cook over a low flame for 25 to 30 minutes, or until firm in the center.

No-Flour Camp Corn Bread

1 1/2 c. cornmeal
1 tsp. salt
1 tsp. baking soda
1 tbsp. sugar, molasses, sorghum, or honey
2 c. buttermilk or sour milk
2 eggs, beaten
1 tbsp. butter or margarine, melted (or other fat)

Mix the dry ingredients. Stir in liquids. Spoon into a well-greased hot 10- or 12-inch skillet. Cover, and cook over a low flame for about 30 minutes or until the corn bread is firm in the center (or bake in the oven at 425° F. for approximately 30 minutes).

Corncakes
(Cornmeal Pancakes)

2 c. cornmeal
2 tbsp. flour
2 tsp. baking powder
3/4 tsp. salt
2 eggs, beaten
1 tbsp. butter or margarine, melted (or other fat)
Milk

    Combine all ingredients, using enough milk to make a thin batter. Pour, by tablespoons, into a hot greased skillet or onto a hot griddle and cook briefly. Turn to brown other side.

    "Pot likker" was a Southern delicacy loved by slaves and whites alike. If Providence provided a ham and cabbage (as in this excerpted letter from South Carolina surgeon Spencer Glasgow Welch, written to his wife from camp near Orange Court House, Virginia, on January 30, 1864), the camp cook could prepare (among other things) a mouth-watering "pot likker."

> *"About ten days ago I succeeded in buying some turnips and cabbage, and I found them most delightful for a change until our box from home arrived. Everything in it was in excellent condition except the sweet potatoes. It contained ten gallons of kraut, ten of molasses, forty pounds of flour, twelve of butter, one-half bushel of Irish potatoes, one-half peck of onions, about one peck of sausage, one ham, one side of bacon and some cabbage."* [24]

    Here are instructions for utilizing some of these edibles in a most worthy manner:

". . . A whole ham, or possibly two, were placed in a big pot of water over the fire. When the meat was partly cooked, cabbages were added, and later peeled potatoes were placed in the pot, and when these vegetables were partly cooked together, they were taken out and a handful of corn meal was sprinkled over the pot liquor and allowed to cook a few minutes. The pot liquor was thus seasoned with juicy, fat ham, scraps of the cabbages, potatoes and corn meal dumplings and thickened with corn meal. It needed no other seasoning, and was superior in flavor and strength of nourishment." [25]

Breads other than corn bread were baked, but shortages of wheat flour sometimes made it necessary to substitute rice flour or rice for part of the flour. At times baking soda and yeast were not to be had. Individuals were issued rations, including flour, to utilize as best they could. Because of lack of equipment, especially when men were on the march, bread-making was sometimes accomplished in the manner described by Timothy Mitchell, writing home to southwest Virginia from Tennessee: "Our flour we make up in an oil cloth, back of a dirty shirt, or towel; roll it 'round a stick and hold it before the fire." [26]

Other standard fare included the aforementioned hardtack (also known as hard bread, ship's bread, sea bread, pilot bread, or sea biscuit). It was not referred to as hardtack until 1861. Tack is a contemptuous term for food. It was merely a thick, virtually imperishable square cracker made of flour and water. When fresh, it is not unappetizing, but when boxes of hardtack sat on railroad platforms or in warehouses for months at a time before being issued to the men, the foodstuff hardened and often became insect-infested.

The following commemorative recipe utilizes rye flour (or a combination of rye and wheat flours) to produce a palatable cracker that has enough of a chewy tough texture to remind one of the Civil War "tooth dullers" or "sheetiron crackers." Because the hardtack was packaged in boxes marked "B. C." (probably for "brigade commissary"), the men took to saying that the crackers were so hard that they must have been baked "before Christ."

The following cracker recipes do not, fortunately, imitate the indestructible character of 19th-century hardtack (some of which was supposedly left over from the 1846-1848 Mexican War). *These* recipes produce tasty crackers, being comprised of more than just flour and water.

Swedish Hardtack

3/4 c. water (approximately)
3 tbsp. vegetable oil
3 tbsp. honey
3 c. rye flour (or 1 1/2 c. rye and 1 1/2 c. whole wheat flour)
1 1/2 tbsp. Brewer's Yeast (nutritional yeast) powder
    (optional)
1/4 tsp. salt

Mix together the liquids. In a separate bowl, mix the dry ingredients. Combine the mixtures, stirring to moisten throughout. Form a ball. On a floured surface, flatten the dough, and roll out thinly. Cut into squares, rectangles, your choice. Prick each cracker with the tines of a fork a couple of times.

Transfer to lightly greased baking sheets. Bake at 425° F. around 8 minutes, checking to be sure not to over-brown. These crackers are best served warm.

Southern Soda Crackers

2 c. flour, preferably whole wheat
1/4 tsp. salt

1/2 tsp. baking soda
2 tbsp. oil
2/3 c. sour milk (or buttermilk)

 Mix dry ingredients. Add oil and sour milk. With a fork, stir to thoroughly moisten. Form a ball. Flatten and roll out on a floured surface. Using a large knife, cut into squares (the dough will look something like an expanded tic-tac-toe grid — the crackers need not be perfectly square!). Using a flat metal "pancake flipper," transfer to baking sheets. Prick crackers with a fork.

 Bake at 350° F. for about 8-10 minutes, watching vigilantly so as not to burn them. They are best served warm. (You may, of course, prepare the crackers ahead of time and re-heat the needed amount at mealtime. We enjoy Southern Soda Crackers along with a tossed salad at the beginning of a meal.)

 The Rev. J. William Jones gave the following account involving the distribution of religious tracts or pamphlets.

> *"My old colonel, now Lieutenant-General A. P. Hill, and one of the most accomplished soldiers, as well as one of the most high-toned gentlemen whom the war produced, pleasantly asked of me, as he gave me a hearty greeting, 'John' (as he always familiarly called me), 'don't you think the boys would prefer "hard-tack" to tracts just now?'*
>
> *"'I have no doubt that many of them would,' I replied; 'but they crowd around and take the tracts as eagerly as they surround the commissary, when he has anything to "issue," and, besides other advantages, the tracts certainly help them to bear the lack of "hard-tack."'"* [27]

Despite its lack of taste appeal, hardtack could be an extremely welcome item, as the following account by Confederate doctor John Claiborne shows:

> ". . . We [two] made a breakfast, as soon as we were awakened by the daylight, from some hard tack which Dr. Field had bought from one of our guards the night before, in exchange for a ring. It had been wrapped in an old handkerchief of the Doctor's which had been innocent of the laundry from some days, [and] was enjoyed with a zest real on that occasion, but difficult to understand at this lapse of time." [28]

On a serious note, the following account concerns General Robert E. Lee in Chambersburg, Pennsylvania, near Gettysburg, in 1863:

> ". . . In a short time I found myself seated by General Lee himself. I stated to him our need, and told him starvation would soon be at hand upon many families unless he gave aid. He seemed startled by this announcement, and said that such destitution seemed impossible in such a rich and beautiful grain-growing country, pointing to the rich fields of grain all around his camp. I reminded him that this growing grain was useless to us now, and that many of our people had no means to lay in supplies ahead. He then assured me that he had turned over the supplies of food he found to his men, to keep them from ravaging our homes. He said, 'God help you if I permitted them to enter your houses. Your supplies depend upon the amount that is sent in to my men.'" [29]

General Lee was constantly concerned about his men. An inscription at Appomattox Court House National Historic

Site quotes him as saying, "I have been up to see the Congress and they do not seem to be able to do anything except eat peanuts and chew tobacco, while my army is starving . . . ."

The aforementioned Rev. Jones also wrote:

> "*General Lee has issued a beautiful address upon the temporary scarcity of rations, and gives example as well as precept. At a dinner to which he was invited the other day, he refused the rich viands with which the table was loaded, and made his dinner off of beef and bread — remarking that he could not consent to be feasting, while there was a scarcity of rations among his men.*" [30]

Timothy Mitchell wrote from Union in Monroe County, West Virginia, in May of 1862:

> "*. . . Crackers and beef without salt. I being far from well could not eat anything and on the 23rd at daylight we got to Lewisburg and commenced cannonading and seeing the Yankee waggons going out of town on the other side and supposing there was but few of the enemy in the place and they would retreat if we would make a charge upon the place, so we was ordered down from a noble position, cannon and all, which if we had of helt we certainly would have whiped them, but Alas! for our misfortune after getting completely caught in their snair their no. being 5700 fresh and rested all under concealment ours [2200] being hungry and broken down and exposed to plain view from every side. In less than one hour we had to leave the field in confusion with a loss of some 400 killed and missing 4 pieces of*

artillery & their baggage or ammunition waggons, & a great many fine horses which was killed upon the field, we fell back across the bridge over Greenbriar River 3 miles & packed hay & old rails upon it & had it in flames by the time the Yankees got there . . . . Had I any way of conveyance I would come home. I am unable to fight or march at present. I have had nothing to eat for 3 days. I cannot eat such diet as we draw it done well enough while I was well, if I was only at home where I could get something that I could eat." [31]

As mentioned, cooking vessels were in short supply (the War has been described as "years of hard marches, 'hardtack,' short fare and short wear — victories and reverses — to the 9th of April at Appomattox" [32]). So many shortages! Yet the men made do, improving, improvising, and substituting as the need arose, as is described by Carlton McCarthy, a private in the Richmond Howitzers:

"Canteens were very useful at times, but they were as a general thing discarded. They were not much used to carry water, but were found useful when the men were driven to the necessity of foraging, for conveying buttermilk, cider, sorghum, etc. to camp. A good strong tin cup was found better than a canteen, as it was easier to fill at a well or spring, and was serviceable as a boiler for making coffee when the column halted for the night." [33]

Dealing with scarcities was the daily routine in the South. A sense of humor did much to distract one from the taste of Confederate Camp Cush, a rather pitiful supper dish.

Cush I (It gets better.)

Fry bits of meat in a skillet. Add water. Thicken with crumbled bread.

Cush II (. . . And progressively better . . .)

To fried, crumbled bacon bits or bacon drippings, add cubed, leftover cooked beef (about 1/4 lb. beef). Add 4 minced garlic cloves. Sauté. Stir in about 1 1/2 cups water. Bring to a boil, stirring frequently. Stir in 1/2 cup cornmeal and salt to taste. Cook, stirring often, until thickened.

Cush III (Gourmet quality!)

1/4 c. butter and/or bacon drippings, or a combination thereof
1/4 c. onion, finely chopped
1 c. biscuit crumbs
2 c. corn bread crumbs
1 tsp. ground sage
Salt and pepper to taste
2 eggs, beaten
Milk

Using a heavy skillet, sauté the onion in the fat. Add crumbs and seasonings and lightly brown the crumbs. Stir in the eggs and sufficient milk to make a thick, mush-like mixture. Set the skillet in a preheated 350° F. oven. Bake for 15-20 minutes. (Or cover and cook over a low flame until firm.) Serve hot.

Bacon drippings were, as is apparent from the preceding recipes, useful for sautéing and for flavoring. Pork fat was also marshalled into use in a rather unusual circumstance in

1862 in Hampton Roads, Virginia. On March 9 of that year the USS Monitor met the CSS Virginia (formerly the USS Merrimac) in the first battle ever waged between ironclad ships. The sides of the "Virginia" were gleaming with a coating of pork fat applied to make cannon shot glance off.[34]

Chicken was also a well-loved meat during the Civil War, but more difficult to obtain than pork or beef. Following are "chicken accounts" from surgeon Spencer Glasgow Welch:

> "I discovered a small chicken roosting in a peach tree and caught it, and Wilson skinned it and broiled it, and it was all we three had to eat that day."[35]
>
> "Edwin and James Allen dined with me yesterday and said it was the best meal they had partaken of since they left home. We had fried tripe, chicken and dumplings, shortened biscuits, tea which was sweetened, and peach pie."[36]
>
> "[My brother] has been keeping a chicken and it is now nearly grown, so we intend to have a big dinner soon, and will make a pot of dumplings and also have stewed corn and Irish potatoes."[37]

More typical were meals such as these:

> "I had my third mess of beans yesterday, and a big one it was too. I shall have rather a poor dinner to-day — only bread, meat and coffee. We have been getting enough coffee and sugar to have it twice a day ever since I got back from home in April."[38]
>
> "I feel fine and have stood the march admirably. We have had plenty of meat and bread

to eat since we started, and I got some good rich milk this morning at Front Royal." [39]

"Camp near Orange Court House, Va. 9/1/63 . . . We are living just as well as we could wish. I bought a bushel of potatoes yesterday, and we have plenty of meal, some flour, one ham and some rice." [40]

"Near Petersburg, Va., October 29, 1864. . . . My dinner will soon be ready and I think it will be fine, for I shall have white cabbage, bacon, potatoes, and biscuit." [41]

On the march, though, the occasional comforts of camp life were left behind: no more peach pies and sweetened tea. "Pocket" food like beef jerky took the place of chicken and dumplings. — Beef jerky can be quite delicious, as the following commemorative recipe demonstrates.

8th Virginia Jerky Recipe

1 lb. lean flank steak (no fat — trim off all fat; cut into thin strips)
1 tbsp. salt
1 tsp. each red pepper, black pepper, and garlic powder
Dash of Liquid Smoke
1/2 to 1 c. water, to cover

Marinate above ingredients overnight. The next day, smoke 6 hours in a covered grill. (The anonymous re-enactor who generously shared with us this recipe and the jerky it produces recommends a Weber kettle: "Use 12 pieces of charcoal and choke the kettle down.")

When on the move, peanuts were a source of nourishment (not always appreciated by the Rebel), as the lyrics to this popular "War for Southern Independence" song indicate:

"Goober Peas"

*"Sitting by the roadside on a summer day,
Chatting with my messmates, passing time away,
Lying in the shadow underneath the trees,
Goodness, how delicious, eating goober peas!*

*(Chorus) "Peas! Peas! Peas! Peas! Eating goober peas!
Goodness, how delicious, eating goober peas!*

*"When a horseman passes, the soldiers have a rule,
To cry out at their loudest, 'Mister, here's your mule,'
But another pleasure enchantinger than these,
Is wearing out your grinders, eating goober peas! (Chorus)*

*"Just before the battle the General hears a row,
He says, 'The Yanks are coming, I hear their rifles now,'
He turns around in wonder, and what do you think he sees?
The Georgia militia eating goober peas! (Chorus)*

*"I think my song has lasted almost long enough,
The subject's interesting, but the rhymes are mighty rough,
I wish this war was over, when free from rags and fleas,
We'd kiss our wives and sweethearts and gobble goober peas!" (Chorus)* [42]

The next modern recipe for Peanut-Pea Salad utilizes peanuts to advantage:

Peanut-Pea Salad

1 10-oz. pkg. frozen green peas, uncooked
1/2 c. Spanish peanuts
1/2 c. celery, diced
Mayonnaise or commercial salad dressing

    Defrost the green peas, but do not cook. Combine the thawed peas with the peanuts, celery, and just enough mayonnaise or salad dressing to hold all of the above ingredients together. Chill. (This is pretty served on lettuce leaves in a menu with roast beef and cooked carrots[43] — the Rebs seldom had it so good!)

    On the subject of salads, the following Timothy Mitchell story somewhat relates to that topic (read and see!):

    ". . . I remind myself of a gentleman that once had an infection of the stomach. [He] went to a Yankee doctor to be cured [and] was told he would have to be surgically operated upon. After receiving a morpheous draught [he] was laid upon the operating bench, [and] his stomach taken out to be cleaned, washed, and rightly adjusted — and laid out upon a stump to dry. While in that condition, a dog came and picked it up, ran off and ate it. The doctor took off after the dog and finding he could not overtake the dog; and thinking if a wooden nutmeg could be put off for genuine, he still could manage the affair handsomely . . . he took off after a sheep and, meeting with better success, gets the sheep's stomach. [He] put it in place of his patient's stomach and closed him up — in due course of time, he recovered entirely and being out one day and meeting with the doctor was asked of his health. 'Well, doctor' says he, 'my health is fine, but ever since you performed that operation upon me I have been eternally a "hankering after grass."'"[44]

    The craving for greens described by Timothy Mitchell may be satisfied with the following recipes.

Wilted Greens
With Sweet/Sour Bacon Dressing

4-6 slices bacon, cut into 1/2" pieces
2 tbsp. cider vinegar
1 tbsp. lemon juice
1 tsp. sugar
1/4 tsp. salt (or to suit taste)
1/2 c. onion, chopped
1 lb. fresh greens (spinach, dandelion, endive, or any other crisp, tart salad greens), torn into bite-sized pieces
1 hard-cooked egg, chopped

In a large skillet, sauté the bacon until crisp. Add other ingredients except for the egg. Stir the fresh greens mixture until the leaves are coated with dressing and just slightly wilted. Put into a serving bowl and sprinkle with chopped egg. Serves 4-6.

"Discovered Garden" Rice

2 tbsp. fat (bacon grease, butter, margarine, or oil)
1 c. onions, chopped
1/2 c. uncooked white rice
Salt and pepper to taste
1 1/2 c. tomatoes, chopped
1 lb. fresh spinach, washed

Heat the fat in a large skillet. Add onions and cook until almost tender. Stir in remaining ingredients. Cover and cook, stirring occasionally, until the rice is tender. (If the mixture gets too dry, add water.)

Fresh fruit was also a much-sought-after commodity. Around Petersburg, Virginia, in autumn 1864 nice peaches cost two to five dollars a dozen, as did apples. A Georgia soldier just back from leave wrote from Petersburg that he was disappointed that he could not have stayed at home for the fall fruit harvest.[45]

During an earlier season of the year Henry Kyd Douglas, a member of Stonewall Jackson's staff, wrote:

> "My breakfast . . . consisted of a piece of beef . . . with hard tack, a tin cup of coffee, and dessert. The dessert was furnished by a sutler's wagon, captured by the cavalry. It consisted of a can of peaches into which I poured a small can of condensed milk and stirred it up with the point of my useful sword. Peaches and cream in January, and furnished by the enemy, too!" [46]

He reported another special meal:

> "About midnight the staff regaled themselves at Woodstock with a heterogeneous supper, furnished by the different sutler stores of General Banks. There were probably too many delicacies of inconsistent qualities to suit the taste of a *bon vivant*, but we had no one with us to make objections. It was indeed a sumptuous table: cake and pickled lobsters, cheese, canned peaches, piccolomini and candy, coffee, ale, and condensed milk. It was feast the like of which was seldom vouchsafed to Confederate soldiers, and with inexpressible thanks we drank the health of General Banks." [47]

On occasion, the hardships of war were lessened by the use of alcoholic beverages. The following recipe is included in *Resources of the Southern Field and Forests*.

Sassafras Beer

"A cheap and wholesome beer for the use of the soldiers, or as a table beer, is prepared from the sassafras, the ingredients being easily obtained. Take eight bottles of *water [in which have been boiled young shoots of sassafras), one quart of molasses, one pint of yeast, one tablespoonful of ginger, one and a half tablespoonfuls of cream of tartar, these ingredients being well stirred and mixed in an open vessel; after standing twenty-four hours the beer may be bottled, and used immediately."* [48]

Sustained by a rollicking sense of humor, perhaps an occasional dipper of "spirits," **SOUTHERN** ingenuity, and trust in the Lord, the Confederate soldier gamely underwent the hardships of war. When men facing battle pinned on strips of paper listing their names, company, and regiment so that they could be identified if killed,[49] we sense the reality of wartime existence. Life fluctuated from days of languid camaraderie in camp to hellish hours of mutilation and slaughter under fire. Just as military action varied, so did a soldier's diet. On February 5, 1863, Charles Blackford speaks of a Captain John L. Cockran's body-servant who became camp chef: an "old man . . . greyhaired with side whiskers, very courtly manners and a fluent vocabulary . . . he is a good cook. Yesterday he supplied us with soup, fritters, and cherry roll, all of which seems to be of the highest grade of gastronomic excellence."[50] And yet in May, in a letter Mrs. Blackford describes her husband's campfire fare as being very plain — salads made up of the young sprouts of the poke-berry, and for variety, small wild onions ("which gave their flavor to all the milk we could get") — comprising part of the menu.[51]

The vicissitudes of war life — may we of this day never experience them, and may we never need to sample the concluding authentic recipe:

Roasted Rat

"The rat must be skinned, cleaned, his head cut off and his body laid upon a square board, the legs stretched to their full extent and secured upon it with small tacks, then baste with bacon fat and roast before a good fire quickly like canvas-back ducks." [52]

Notes

[1] W. R. Pendleton, "Personal Recollections of General Lee," *Southern Magazine*, XV (1874), pp. 620-621, quoted in Henry Steele Commager, ed., *The Blue and the Gray*, Bobbs-Merrill, New York, 1950, p. 1067.

[2] Timothy Elijah Mitchell, 1st Sgt., Co. F, 8th Virginia Cavalry, unpublished letter written while "on picquet near Rafaelville, Tennessee," December 12, 1863, to his wife Ardelia (Wohlford) in southwest Virginia (letter provided by their granddaughter Frances Ardelia Buford of Taylors, SC).

[3] A. A. Hoehling and Mary Hoehling, *The Day Richmond Died*, A. S. Barnes & Co., Inc., San Diego and New York, 1981, p. 41.

[4] "Master Biscuit Mix" recipe first published in Patricia B. Mitchell, *Well, Bless Your Heart, Vol. I*, 1989, p. 16.

[5] Susan Leigh Blackford, *Letters from Lee's Army*, Charles Scribner's Sons, New York, 1947, p. 128.

[6] *Ibid.*, pp. 10-11.

[7] *Ibid.*, pp. 173-174.

[8] *Ibid.*, pp. 295-296.

[9] Robert L. Scribner, "Inflation in the 'Good Old Days,'" *Virginia Cavalcade*, Summer 1954, p. 17.

[10] James J. McDonald, *Life in Old Virginia*, The Old Virginia Publishing Co., Inc., Norfolk, VA, 1907, p. 327.

[11] John Herbert Claiborne, A. M., M. D., *Seventy-Five Years in Old Virginia*, The Neale Publishing Co., New York and Washington, 1904, pp. 201-202.

[12] Charles P. Roland, *The Confederacy*, The University of Chicago Press, Chicago, 1960, p. 137.

[13] Blackford, p. 252.

[14] Don Dooley, ed., *Better Homes and Gardens Heritage Cook Book*, Meredith Corp., 1975, p. 151.

[15] Attributed to "Mrs. R. E." in Marion Cabell Tyree, *Housekeeping in Old Virginia*, John P. Morton and Company, Louisville, 1879, p. 84.

[16] Tyree, p. 99.

[17] Egbert L. Viele, *Handbook for Active Service for the Use of Volunteers*, 1861, reprinted by Greenwood Press, New York, p. 83.

[18] Attributed to "Mozis Addums" in Tyree, p. 254.

[19] Attributed to "Mrs. Col. W." in Tyree, p. 254.

[20] Burke Davis, *Our Incredible Civil War*, Holt, Rinehart and Winston, New York, 1960, p. 124.

[21] Francis P. Porcher, *Resources of the Southern Fields and Forests*, 1863, p. 549.

[22] James Trayer, *Foodbook*, Grossman Publishers, New York, 1970, p. 517.

[23] John T. Wickersham, quoted in B. A. Botkin, *A Civil War Treasury*, Promontory Press, New York, 1981, p. 551.

[24] Spencer Glasgow Welch, *A Confederate Surgeon's Letters to*

[24] *His Wife*, The Neale Publishing Company, New York and Washington, 1911, pp. 88-89.

[25] MacDonald, p. 235.

[26] Timothy E. Mitchell (see footnote 2).

[27] J. William Jones, D. D., *Christ in the Camp, or Religion in the Confederate Army*, B. F. Johnson & Co., 1887, reprinted by The Martin & Hoyt Co., Atlanta, GA, 1904, p. 53.

[28] Claiborne, p. 294.

[29] Ellen McLellan, quoted in Botkin, pp. 261-262.

[30] Jones, p. 359.

[31] Timothy E. Mitchell, unpublished letter written from Union, Monroe County, [West] Virginia, May 26, 1862, to his wife Ardelia (letter provided by their great-grandsons Garnet and Wilbur Strock, Bland County, VA).

[32] Botkin, p. 148.

[33] Carlton McCarthy, *Detailed Minutiae of Soldier Life in the Army of Northern Virginia, 1861-1865*, Carlton McCarthy & Co., Richmond, 1882, pp. 16-28; quoted in Commager, p. 281.

[34] John D. Broadwater, "Ironclad at Hampton Roads," *Virginia Cavalcade* magazine, Winter 1984, p. 109.

[35] Welch, p. 29.

[36] *Ibid.*, p. 40.

[37] *Ibid.*, p. 85.

[38] *Ibid.*, p. 101.

[39] *Ibid.*, p. 56.

[40] *Ibid.*, p. 77.

[41] *Ibid.*, p. 113.

[42] A. Pender, quoted in Commager, pp. 584-585.

[43] Recipe courtesy Mary Ruth Edwards, Chatham, VA.

[44] Timothy E. Mitchell, unpublished letter written from Copper Valley, Giles County, Virginia to his mother-in-law Elizabeth Nicewander (Mrs. Samuel) Wohlford (letter provided by his grandson J. T. W. Mitchell of Bristol, TN).

[45] Reid Mitchell, *Civil War Soldiers*, Viking Penguin Inc., New York, 1988, p. 167.

[46] Henry Kyd Douglas, *I Rode with Stonewall*, The University of North Carolina Press, Chapel Hill, 1940, p. 23.

[47] *Ibid.*, p. 71.

[48] Porcher, p. 343.

[49] Blackford, p. 104.

[50] *Ibid.*, p. 166.

[51] *Ibid.*, p. 172.

[52] Phoebe Yates Pember, superintendent of one of the wings of Richmond's Chimborazo Hospital, quoted in Botkin, p. 148.